GRADE 1 HISTORY: LEARNING AND DISCOVERY FOR KIDS

Speedy Publishing LLC
40 E. Main St. #1156
Newark, DE 19711
www.speedypublishing.com

AMERICAN HISTORY
FUN FACTS

The Declaration of Independence was signed on July 4, 1776.

The first shots of the Civil War were fired at Fort Sumter, in South Carolina.

A **tariff** is a tax on goods brought into a country.

A Republic is a nation in which voters choose representatives to govern them.

Federalism is the sharing of power between the states and the national government.

Ratify means to approve by vote.

The Constitution of the United States was written in 1787.

The Civil War was fought from 1861-1865.

Jamestown, the first permanent English settlement, was founded in 1607.

The Battle of Saratoga was the turning point of the American Revolution.

Concord, Massachusetts was the site of the first battle of the American Revolution.

Sectionalism is a strong sense of loyalty to a state or section instead of to the whole country.

The House of Burgesses was the first representative assembly in the new world.

WORLD HISTORY FUN FACTS

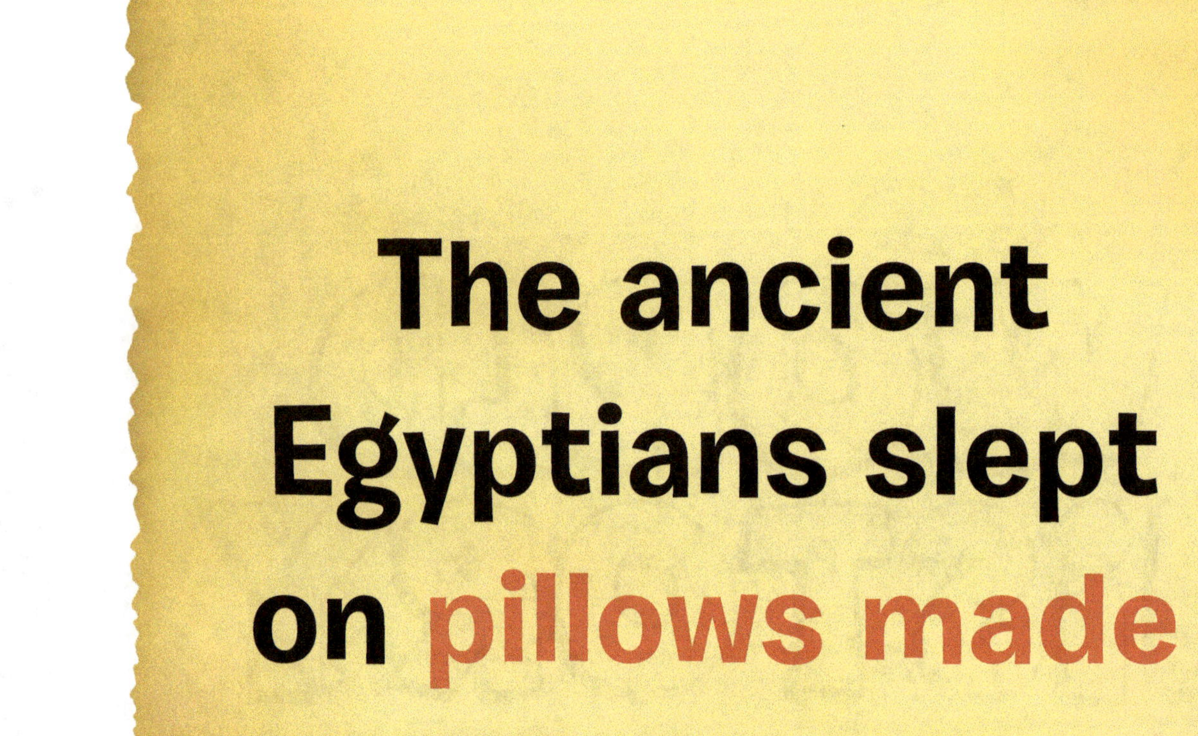

The ancient Egyptians slept on pillows made of stone.

The Hundred Years War actually lasted 116 years (1337 to 1453).

Roman Emperor Caligula made his horse, Inciatus, an official Senator of Rome.

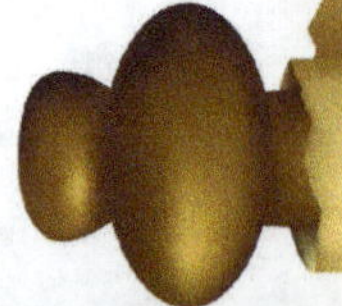

There are 92 known cases of nuclear bombs lost at sea.

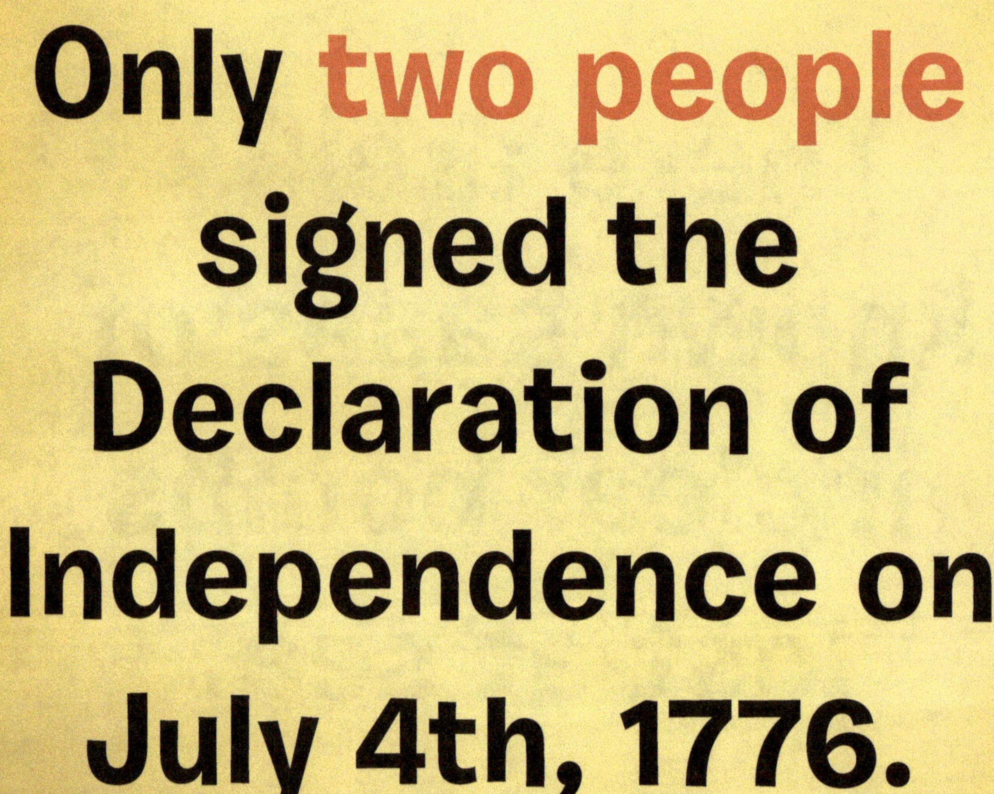
Only two people
signed the
Declaration of
Independence on
July 4th, 1776.

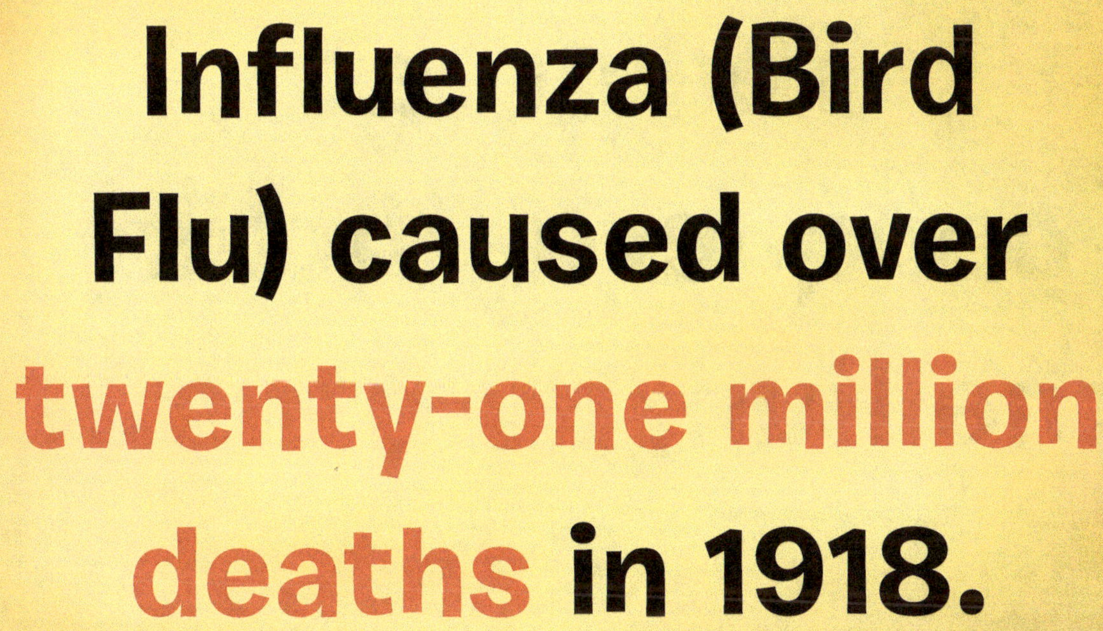
Influenza (Bird
Flu) caused over
twenty-one million
deaths in 1918.

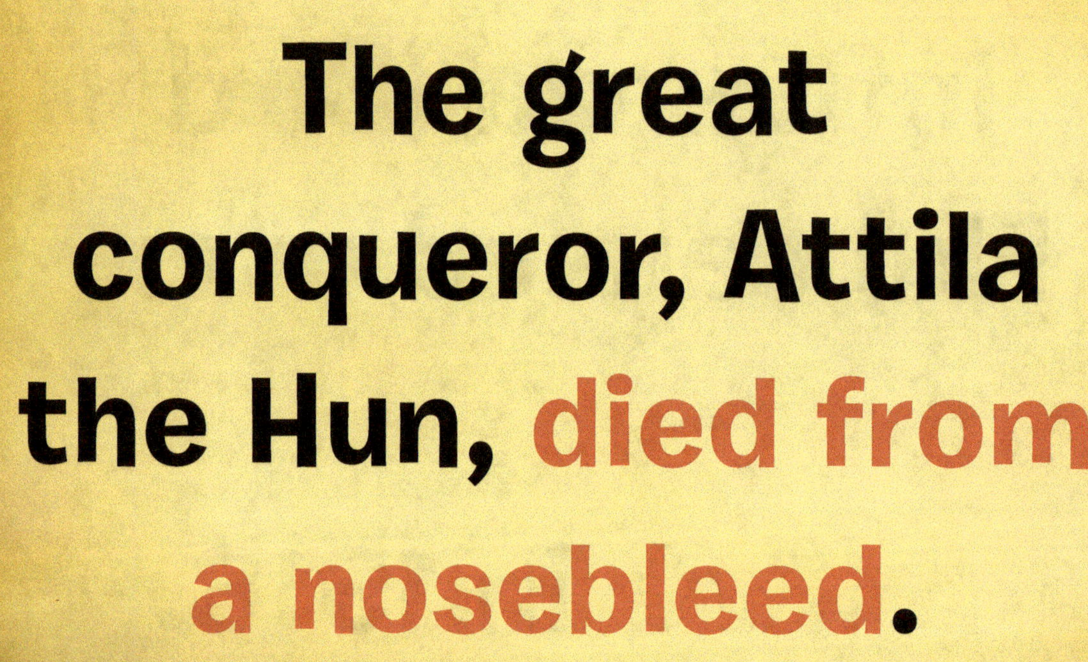

The great conqueror, Attila the Hun, died from a nosebleed.

Cleopatra married two of her brothers.

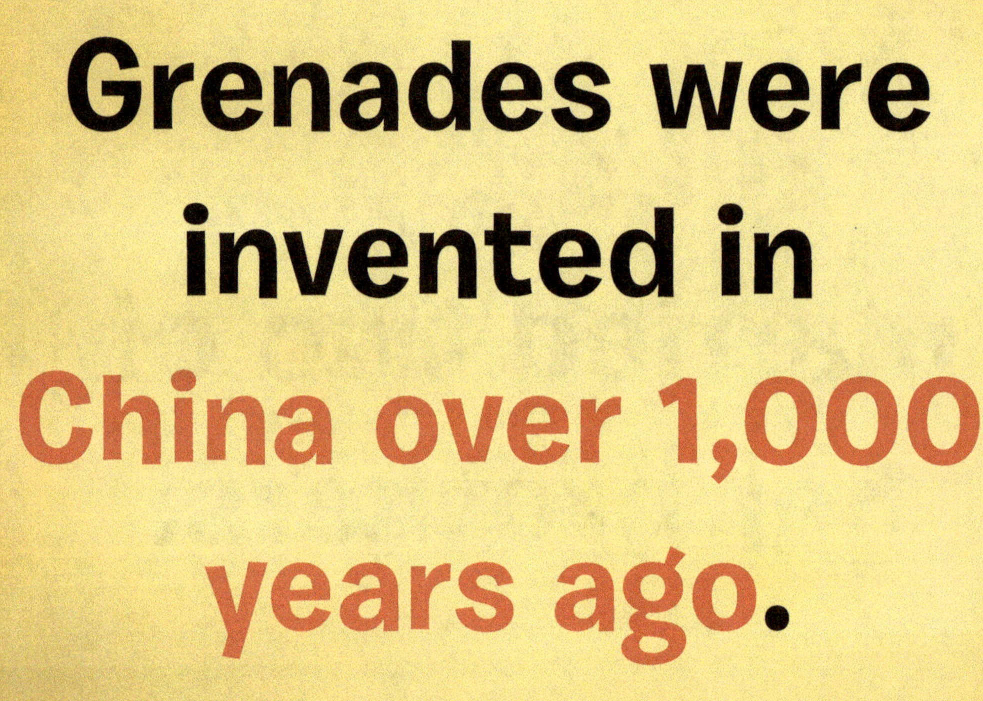

Grenades were invented in China over 1,000 years ago.

It is rumored that Adolph Hitler's grandmother was Jewish.

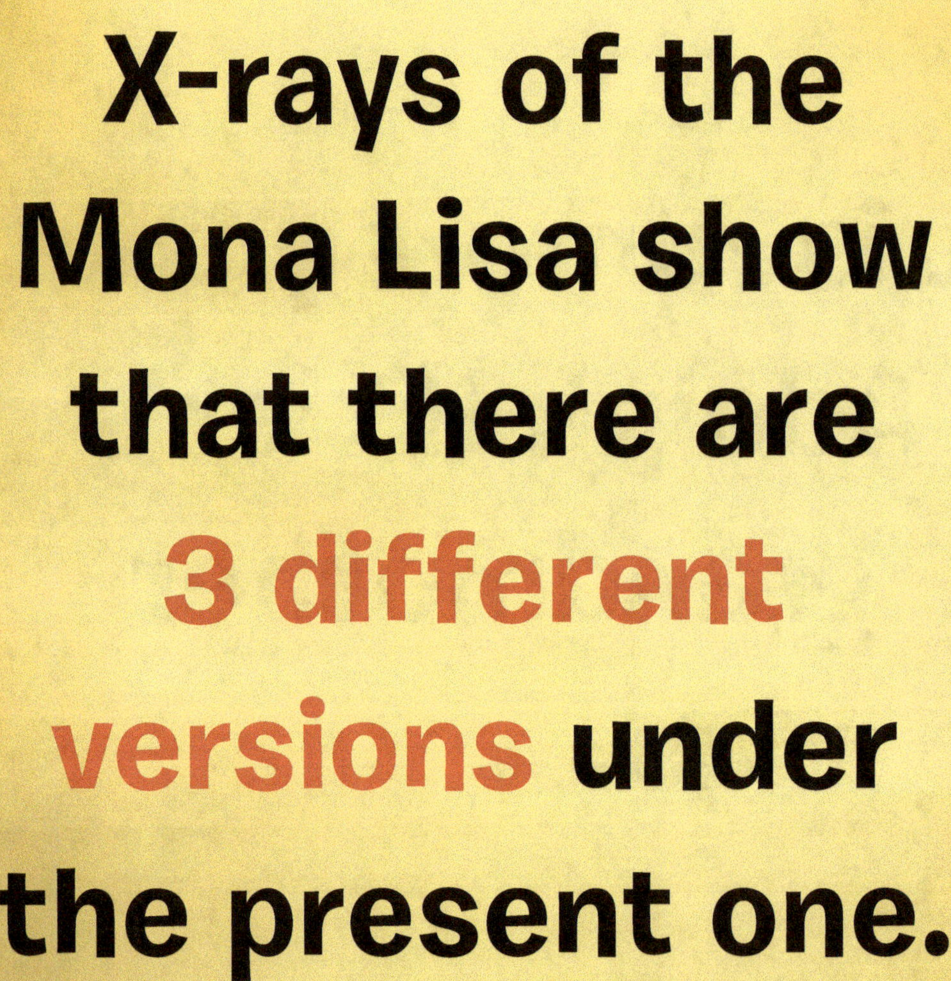
X-rays of the
Mona Lisa show
that there are
3 different
versions under
the present one.

Members of the Nazi SS had their blood type tattooed on their armpits.

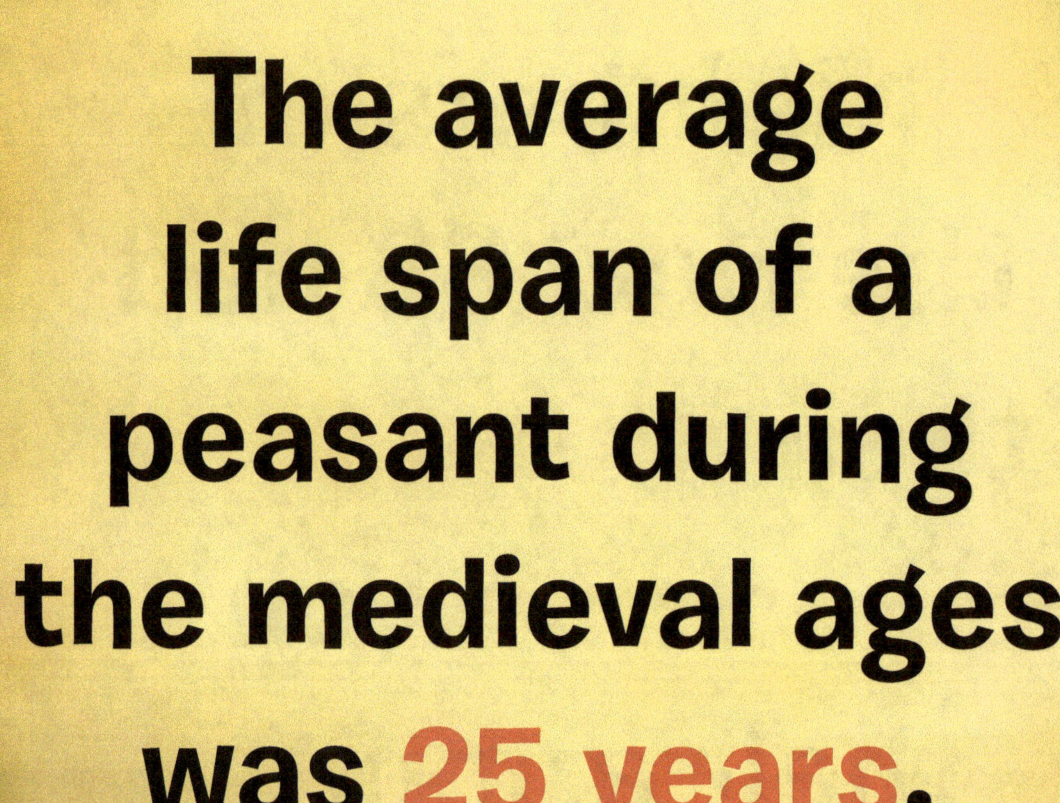
The average
life span of a
peasant during
the medieval ages
was 25 years.

In ancient Egypt, people **shaved their eyebrows** as a mourning symbol when their cats died.

www.ingramcontent.com/pod-product-compliance
Lightning Source LLC
LaVergne TN
LVHW060833170826
845678LV00010B/1970

* 9 7 9 8 8 6 9 4 5 3 7 8 5 *